Poetry...A Song From My Heart

Judith Asmus Hill

America Star Books

First printing

Softcover 9781633825567
PUBLISHED BY AMERICA STAR BOOKS, LLLP
www.americastarbooks.com

DEDICATION

I dedicate this fourth book of poetry to all of those who want to have God's song in their heart. Those who have wounded hearts and are looking for a deep healing: I dedicate every poem and scripture to YOU! To all of you who will do your part to help others find the healing love of JESUS, I dedicate this book, "POETRY .... A SONG FROM MY HEART!"
Sending you love from my heart to yours,

Judy

ACKNOWLEDGEMENTS

I would like to honor and thank my precious Lord and Savior, Jesus Christ for saving my soul and bringing a song into my heart!

I am forever grateful for my awesome husband, Jim, for doing extra things around our home, with a joyful heart, so that I could have the time to write and complete this work!

Jim brings a song to my heart because He loves Jesus and that is why I could bring *"POETRY ... A SONG FROM MY HEART,"* to fruition!

I am very thankful that my children and grandchildren love the Lord and understand the time it takes to complete a poetry book, while keeping up with family events and singing/ministry appointments.

I would also like to thank WLMB TV for asking me to read my poetry and scripture throughout the day on our Local Hometown Christian TV Station! I am thankful to all of you who have encouraged me by letting me know that you are blessed by, *"MOMENTS OF GRACE,"* the one minute spots that are aired on WLMB TV.

TABLE OF CONTENTS

A PEACEFUL PLACE

There are times when life gets crazy
Your plans for life seem so hazy.

I pull back to get away
To find a peaceful place each day.

A time to read God's Word and pray
Surely He will show the way.

When dreams are shattered and life is tough
Keep looking to JESUS, He's more than enough.

His arms are open; sees every tear
Let His Word revive you from all of your fear.

Pray without ceasing. In everything give thanks: for this is the will of God in Christ Jesus concerning you.
1 Thessalonians 5:17, 18

Let my supplication come before thee: deliver me according to thy word.
Psalm 119:170

AN OBJECT LESSON JUST FOR ME

We were outside in God's lovely creation
It speaks to me encouragement and imagination.

Right beside my chair, a little ways away
Was a cute little gecko taking a long stay.

He started doing push-ups: four in a row
He waited a long time, didn't move, and didn't go.

It was so unusual; I knew that God was talking
An object lesson just for me, to help in my life's walking.

When we face a storm, our spirit exercises
Then we call on God and wait 'til help arises.

If we take the time to notice, there are signs everywhere
God shows us things in nature about His loving care.

My soul, wait thou only upon God; for my expectation is from Him.

PSALM 62:5

I will be glad and rejoice in thy mercy: for thou hast considered my trouble; thou hast known my soul in adversities.

Psalm 31:7

BE SURE TO TAKE TIME

In the twinkling of a moment
You can be…
Back in your childhood
Look and see.

I remember the time
Along the river bank
My dad took me fishing
I forgot to thank.

I forgot to thank him
When older I grew…
For those special moments
I hope he knew.

Be sure to take time
Those memories to make
Childhood passes quickly
Do it for their sake.

Children's children are the crown of old men. And the glory
of children are their fathers.

Proverbs 17:6

Redeeming the time, because the days are evil.

Ephesians 5:16

BRINGS MY EYES TO TEARS

So many friends on Facebook
Writing out their posts
You can tell a lot about a person
What in whom he boasts.

You can tell where their love is
And the things that make them sing
It sometimes surprises you
And makes your ears to ring.

The books they read, movies they watch
Language that appears…
Many times it actually
Brings my eyes to tears.

We're in a generation
That's been desensitized
Help us Lord to follow You
Even if we're criticized,

Let another man praise thee, and not thine own mouth; a
stranger, and not thine own lips.

Proverbs 27:2

Your glorying is not good. Know ye not that a little leaven
leaveneth the whole lump?

1 Corinthians 5:6

CLOSE TO DEATH

They called code blue, you don't even know
You were close to death, which way will you go?

When you awake, faces looking on
What are you thinking; you could have been gone.

Things look different, priorities change
Time to ask God to help rearrange.

Many things don't matter, when you're at death's door
All you need is Jesus and what He has in store.

The Lord knoweth the days of the upright: and their inheritance shall be forever.

Psalm 37:18

Wait on the Lord, and keep His way, and He shall exalt thee to inherit the land: when the wicked are cut off, thou shalt see it.

Psalm 37:34

DID I PLEASE YOU LORD

The sun left our sky for another day
Did I please you Lord in what I had to say?

I want to live each day to bring you glory
If I go my own way, it's a different story.

Thank you Lord, for the beauty of creation
It lives in my heart with Your inspiration.

The time is near for Your returning
Looking to You with intense yearning.

Not unto us, O Lord, not unto us, but unto Thy name give glory, for Thy mercy, and for Thy truth's sake.

Psalm 115:1

Set a watch, O Lord, before my mouth; keep the door of my lips.

Psalm 141:3

DISCERN THE TIMES

The grains are falling in the hour glass
Discern the times, it's soon to pass.

Are we ready, our Lord, to meet
Be careful the way, you walk your feet.

The things we watch and the books we read
Will surely affect our every need.

Jesus will come like a thief in the night
Will you be ready for your flight?

Make the most of every day...
Only God's Word can show the way.

The night is far spent, the day is at hand: let us therefore cast off the works of darkness, and let us put on the armour of light.

Romans 13:12

For yourselves know perfectly that the day of the Lord so cometh as a thief in the night. Ye are all the children of light, and the children of the day: we are not of the night, nor of darkness.

1 Thessalonians 5:2, 5

DYING TO SELF

Dying to self is a process
That no one likes to go through
There's sadness and crying
And maybe some anger, too.

When the Lord reveals
Our selfish heart...
He's there with forgiveness
A brand new start.

A smile returns
A load is lifted
When you know you've done right
The weight has shifted.

His yoke is easy
His burden is light
He's there to help
In day or night.

If any man will come after me, let him deny himself, and take up his cross daily and follow me.

Luke 9:23

My yoke is easy, and my burden is light.

Matthew 11:30

FRIENDS ARE SO PRECIOUS

As night falls again, another day has past
Many friends to see from the time before last.

Friends are so precious, a joy to find
It warms your heart because they're so kind.

When friends move away and you feel alone
Remember God's plan, He's on the throne.

Things may change, moments may fly
Jesus never changes, always standing by.

Waiting to help us in all that we do
Whatever may happen, He will see us through.

A man who has friends must himself be friendly, but there is a friend that sticks closer than a brother.

Proverbs 18:24

I am a companion of all them that fear thee, and of them that keep thy precepts.

Psalm 119:63

FRIENDSHIP IS GODS WAY

Many times in life, you have been wounded
And you think you can't reach out anymore
Do not be afraid, my child, says Jesus...
I'll be there when you open your hearts door.

Friendship is God's way of loving you
So don't let hurts get in the way
Help a wound be healed quickly
Give God's love and forgiveness today.

Two are better than one you see
If you fall there'd be someone there
Take the time to mend a heart
And let them know you care.

There is something about God's love
Where nothing else comes through
So pray and obey whatever the cost
It's friendship's worth; tried and true.

Two are better than one; because they have a good reward for their labour.

For if they fall, the one will lift up his fellow: but woe to him that is alone when he falleth; for he hath not another to help him up.

Ecclesiastes 4:9, 10

GOD CAN HELP

There is nothing like a sunrise
To take your breath away
To give God your praise
For a beautiful new day.

Before my feet hit the floor
I thanked Him for His goodness
Asked His help for family
Against the Devil's shrewdness.

It's great to know God's always there
He can help with every care
For God, there's nothing He can't do
Ask for His help and He'll be there for you.

Casting all your care upon him; for he careth for you.

1 Peter 5:7

God is our refuge and our strength, a very present help in trouble.

Psalm 46:1

GOD GIVES US FRIENDS

When your heart is lonely and things go wrong
Look to others to help you be strong.

Don't be afraid to call on a friend
Ask first of God and He will send

He will send you ones that really care
There's strength in unity it's always there.

So just like Palm Trees standing together
God gives us friends in stormy weather.

So be there for those that need a hand
Lift them up and help them stand.

A friend loveth at all times, and a brother is born for adversity.

Proverbs 17:17

Thou shalt love thy neighbor as thyself.

Matthew 22:39b

GOD MAY BE PREPARING

Sometimes the sun is shining, but your fence is broken down
You try to have a smile, but it turns into a frown.

You look across the way and see another's fence is standing
Then you're wondering if God's giving reprimanding.

Do not be comparing, just know the Lord is working
The fence will be mended if your trust in God's not shirking.

God may be preparing you for ministry down the road
He does that with his staff and surely with His goad.

Make me to understand the way of thy precepts: so shall I
talk of thy wondrous works.

Psalm 119:27

Thy word is true from the beginning: and every one of thy
righteous judgments endureth for ever.

Psalm 119:160

GOD'S SONG FROM ABOVE

The beauty of God's hand is awesome to see
The fragrance of flowers, the waves of the sea.

The song of the robin, coming back in the spring
After the storm, how much joy it can bring.

But nothing is better, than to know God's love
Deep in your heart, God's song from above.

Ask Him today, to forgive your sin
Open your heart and let Jesus in.

For all have sinned and come short of the glory of God.
Romans 3:23

But God commendeth His love toward us, in that while we were yet sinners, Christ died for us.
Romans 5:8

For the Lord thy God in the midst of thee is mighty; He will save, He will rejoice over thee with joy; He will rest in His love, He will joy over thee with singing.
Zephaniah 3:17

GOD'S TIMEING IS PERFECT

We are so excited for spring to come, the tulips explode with glee
When the robins return and sing their sweet song, it truly sets
our hearts free.

Buds on dead branches burst fragrant bloom
It lifts our spirits, dispels the gloom.

The same thing happens when a trial has past
It seemed like forever that it would last.

God's timing is perfect, if we cooperate
The time of springing forth, we then celebrate.

For, lo, the winter is past, the rain is over and gone; the
flowers appear on the earth; the time of the singing of birds is
come, and the voice of the turtle is heard in our land.

Song of Solomon 2:11, 12

To everything there is a season, and a time to every purpose
under the Heaven.

Ecclesiastes 3:1

HE PAID THE PRICE

Storms and trials come into my life
Don't know at times how to handle the strife.

If I didn't know Jesus as my dearest friend
My fears would control me to the end.

But I've read my Bible
And I know we win.

There's eternity waiting
He paid the price for sin.

For the wages of sin is death; but the gift of God is eternal
life through Jesus Christ our Lord.

Romans 6:23

But they that wait upon the Lord shall renew their strength;
they shall mount up with wings as eagles; they shall run, and
not be weary; and they shall walk, and not faint.

Isaiah 40:31

HIS FOOTPRINTS ALONE

When each step that you take seems too heavy to bear
You think you're done in with worry and care.

You call out to God, He's there and has been
His footprints alone; He carries you then.

Remember nothing can come to you
Unless God allows for His purpose so true.

Footprints are in the sand of your life
Know that He carries you above all the strife.

The Lord is my strength and my shield; my heart trusted in
Him, and I am helped: therefore my heart greatly rejoices; and
with my song I will praise Him. The Lord is their strength and
He is the saving strength of His anointed.

Psalm 28:7-8

O Lord of hosts, blessed is the man that trusts in you.

Psalm 84:12

I CAN'T BE TOO BUSY

Waking up in the morning in our bed
Many thoughts begin to fill my head.

I remember the prayers that I prayed at sunset
Looking over the fields where my eyes met...

My eyes met God's beauty and caring you see
The prayers that I lifted for others in needs.

So many with sorrow and burdens of day
I wanted to help them: I began to pray.

I can't be too busy to care about others
I will take time to pray for sisters and brothers...

This old world is changing, the times drawing near
I will go to the Bible, and pray without fear.

Now the Lord of peace himself give you peace always by all means. The Lord be with you all. The grace of our Lord Jesus Christ be with you all. Amen.

11 Thessalonians 3:16, 18

I KNOW YOUR TIMING'S PERFECT

Remember the time that you ran ahead of God's plan
Thought you had a better way; full steam you ran.

Then you found some trouble; asked God to get you out
He waited for you to come around, and give Him a shout.

A shout of, "Help me Lord, forgive me, for going my way
I know Your timing's perfect, at Your side, I want to stay.

I will follow in Your footsteps, until you make it clear…
Help me to know that in Your Word, I will hear.

Order my steps in Your Word: and let not iniquity have dominion over me.

Psalm 119:133

And your ears shall hear a Word behind you, saying, this is the way, walk ye in it, when ye turn to the right hand, and when ye turn to the left.

Isaiah 30:21

I LOOKED FOR A RAINBOW

I looked for a rainbow today, as the sun shown through the rain
But I couldn't seem to find one, looking out my window pane.

Later I saw a sunset that made me think of God
He is there to remind us as the flowers push through the sod.

When no rainbow fills the sky, His promises are still true
Don't give up on His mighty Word, or the things He's promised
   you.

And whatsoever we ask, we receive of him, because we
keep His commandments, and do those things that are pleasing
in His sight.

1 John 3:22

The eyes of all wait upon thee; and thou givest them their
meat in due season. Thou openest thine hand, and satisfiest the
desire of every living thing.

Psalm 145:15, 16

IF THERE'S AN IDOL

What we think about
Most in our day
Whatever is our focus
That will grow and stay.

If we aren't careful
An idol there will be
Take a day; be watchful
Be aware and see.

Unto our Lord, each morning
Our first thought should be
One of great thanksgiving
So God can help us see.

Inside of our heart
If there's an idol to be
Give us the truth...
Where we need to be free.

Wherefore, my dearly beloved, flee from idolatry.
1 Corinthians 10:14

Thou shalt have no other gods before me.
Exodus 20:3

IF WE WILL JUST BELIEVE

When you are going through a trial
Looking for to see...
Keep your eyes on Jesus
It's the only way to be.

We always want a miracle
But it's a process, often...
Knowing God allowed it
Then the blow will soften.

He is in control
If we will just believe...
He counts it as righteousness
In blessings we'll receive.

My soul, wait thou only upon God; for my expectation is
from him.
He only is my rock and my salvation: I shall not be moved.
Psalm 62:5

Our soul waiteth for the Lord: he is our help and our shield.
Psalm 33:20

IT'S HARD TO KEEP A SMILE

It seems like there are days
That many things go wrong
It's hard to keep a smile
Or even sing a song.

You lost your phone
Your credit card, too
O, Lord please help
I'm in a stew.

It's in these times of testing
God shows what's in my heart
Do I get filled with madness
Or let God do His part.

Sometimes it is the little things
That take away my peace
I must keep my eyes on Him
To help my anger cease.

Please help me, Lord, to come to You
And tell you of my woe...
Then You can come into my heart
And make me truly whole.

Catch us the foxes, the little foxes that spoil the vines,
For our vines have tender grapes.
SONG OF SOLOMON 2:15

Thou wilt keep him in perfect peace, whose mind is stayed
on Thee, because he trusteth in Thee.
ISAIAH 26:3

LABOUR OF LOVE

Stories to tell from a barn inside
Days of hard work, tractors to ride.
Labor of love for the whole family
Bring in the crops, rest under a tree.

We used to hoe in the fields of corn
Made our 3 children tired and worn
Living close to an old barn that's near
Precious memories that brings a tear.

Sometimes we complain for work that we do
But when work is done, rewards will come through.
Our sermon on Sunday said, "Grumble not"
Persevere with God's help though it may take a lot.

In all labour, there is profit:

Proverbs 14:23

For thou shalt eat the labour of thine hands: happy shalt thou be, and it shall be well with thee.

Psalm 128:2

LISTENING IS HARD TO DO

Listening is something that's hard to do
We'd rather be talking about what's new.

It can be draining when others share
But it's so important that you really care.

When you listen to others with a loving heart
You will surely help Jesus do His part.

He works through people, who give of their love
He'll give them blessings from above.

Bear ye one another's burdens, and so fulfil the law of Christ.

Galatians 6:2

Seeing ye have purified your souls in obeying the truth through the Spirit unto unfeigned love of the brethren, see that ye love one another with a pure heart fervently:

1 Peter 1:22

LORD HELP ME TRUST YOU MORE

Rain slides down our window pane
My eyes can clearly see.

Another month has passed
I wonder what will be.

What will happen in this month
Will it be life changing.

Lord, help me trust You more
For every rearranging.

And thine ears shall hear a word behind thee, saying, this
is the way, walk ye in it, when ye turn to the right hand, and
when ye turn to the left.

Isaiah 30:21

For God hath not given us the spirit of fear; but of power,
and of love, and of a sound mind.

11 Timothy 1:7

MY HEART

What I am made of is in my heart
If my trust is in Jesus, He'll do His part.

My heart is deceitful and full of pride
If Jesus is not invited inside.

Jesus came to free me from pride
Because on the cross He freely died.

That is why God's Son hung on a tree
If I believe and repent, I will be free...

I want to tell others who are in pain
Accept Jesus and heaven is your gain.

For God so loved the world, that He gave His only begotten Son, that whosoever believeth in Him should not perish, but have everlasting life.

John 3:16

The heart is deceitful above all things, and desperately wicked: who can know it?

Jeremiah 17:9

MY HEARTFELT CRY

My heart is crying for an answer to be
Which way to go, how can I see.

Different voices tell different things
How do I know the true song that sings.

When stories don't match, who's to believe
I just want the truth, that I can receive.

So I get on my knees and seek God's face
He has the answer that I will embrace.

My soul, wait thou only upon God; for my expectation is from Him.

Psalm 62:5

Wait on the Lord: be of good courage, and He shall strengthen thine heart: wait, I say, on the Lord.

Psalm 27:14

MY SWEET DAUGHTER

My sweet daughter is so special to me
The day she was born, God meant it to be.
She has brought me joy day in and day out
Her smile warms my heart; makes me shout.

From pabulum to braids; and ribbons to gowns
Her heart has been right, even through frowns.
A song in her heart has always been there...
God gifted her voice, so that she could share.

She shares her song of what God has done
Because she has opened her heart to His Son.
She wants to put Jesus first in her life
She knows He is helping her in all strife.

My daughter; a wife and mother of four
God has blessed her even more.
After her Lord, her family is next
The Word of God is her guiding text.

Strength and honor are her clothing: and she shall rejoice
In time to come. She openeth her mouth with wisdom and
In her tongue is the law of kindness. She looketh well to the
Ways of her household and eateth not the bread of idleness.
Her children arise up and call her blessed: her husband also,
And he praiseth her.

Proverbs 31:25-28

NOTHING SO GREAT

Nothing so great as being a mother
Training and guiding like no other.

From labor room to college dorm
Helping them to weather each storm.

Thank you Lord, for giving to me
The blessing of Motherhood, helping them see.

Letting them know that the only way
Is to walk with Jesus every day!

And all thy children shall be taught of the Lord; and great
shall be the peace of thy children.

Isaiah 54:13

Train up a child in the way that he should go: and when he
is old, he will not depart from it.

Proverbs 22:6

OBEY MY WORD

When life looks hopeless
So many things to do
Don not fear, do not doubt
I'll come through for you.

I am your shield and buckler
I'll make my way so clear
Go to my Word and ask of me
For I am very near.

If you never had to trust Me
For the big things in your life
You'd never grow in patience
When life has dealt you strife.

So obey My Word
Anytime day or night
I am always there
To help you in the fight.

Obedience is better than sacrifice.

1 Samuel 15:22b

The Lord shall fight for you, and ye shall hold your peace.

Exodus14:14

OUR PRAYERS MAKE A DIFFERENCE

Soon it will be planting time
And the corn will grow...
God promised seedtime
And harvest, you know.

I love to see the sunset
On the fields of grain...
As a farm girl, my dad
Prayed for sunshine and rain.

Each day is a reminder
When the sun leaves the sky
That we should pray for souls
For the sweet by and by.

Time is so short
And many don't believe
Our prayers can make a difference
And help them to receive.

The prayer of the upright is His delight.

Proverbs 15:8b

But the end of all things is at hand: be ye therefore sober, and watch unto prayer.

1 Peter 4:7

PRAYERS FOR GRACE

Riding in a car on our way home
Many things I notice as we swiftly roam.

I see drivers taking chances
Others watching, staring glances.

Selfish drivers take their paces
Tooting horns and angry faces.

Prayers for grace and angels there
Lord, I know we're in Your care.

Nothing will happen unless you allow
To your wonderful plan, I surely will bow.

He that dwelleth in the secret place of the most High shall abide under the shadow of the Almighty.

Psalm 91:1

For he shall give his angels charge over thee, to keep thee in all thy ways. They shall bear thee up in their hands, lest thou dash thy foot against a stone.

Psalm 91:11, 12

SOME WILL FACE A TRIAL

At the end of a beautiful day
The sun sets in the west.

I pray, O Lord, for the coming weeks
I know You'll do Your best.

And when the sun rises to face another day...
You'll be there with joy and peace to help in every way.

Some will face a trial like never before
But You'll be there to lead, as they face the open door.

We are never alone, You stand by our side
Your loving hand reaches to be our guide.

The Lord is good, a stronghold in the day of trouble.

Nahum 1:7

Let not your heart be troubled: ye believe in God, believe in me.

John 14:1

This is the cover photo of our latest CD" "GENERATIONS
GIVING GOD GLORY!"
Judy is singing with her daughter & 3 granddaughters.

Judy & her family at the recording studio with John Kuser.,
our producer for our latest album, "GENERATIONS GIVING
GOD GLORY!"

Judy's first grandchild's marriage…Mr. & Mrs. Jaryd
Motsinger, May 25, 2013 (Bottom pic), with her daughter,
Beth, husband Kurt, Jim & Judy. Judy's second grandchild,
Stephanie Motsinger, married Luke Humphries on May 11,
2014, here in Ohio, and then again in England, on May 17,
2014.

Jim & Judy in front of the Tower of London Building in London, England, during our trip in May 2014, for our granddaughter's England Wedding.

Everyone is smiling because our Local Christian TV Station WLMB exceeded our Share-a-then Goal! From Right to left... Jamey Schmitz—Pres., & CEO; Judy—Share-a-thon Co-Host; Virginia Bossa—VP Public Relations; Jeff Millslagle—VP Operations & Programming

48

2 years ago, at the request of WLMB TV, their TV Cameras came to Judy & Jim's Log Home to film the segments that are aired on WLMB throughout their Daily Broadcasting. Judy reads her poetry & scripture in one minute segments, which are called, "MOMENTS OF GRACE!"

This was where Judy recorded her CD, "SINGING THE WORD, in Sept. of 2005. Their friend, Dick Dewese, brought the recording studio to their Log Home, when Dean, Judy's first husband was home bound, with 3 lung diseases. Judy recorded this just for Dean & others in severe trials. He graduated to heaven on Feb. 2, 2006.

Judy singing with the Ensemble of the Michigan/Ohio Choir,
where she & Dean sang for almost 20 years.

Judy & Dean, when they took part in an Easter Musical at
their church.

Judy & Dean, when they took part in "THE GOSPEL ACCORDING TO SROOGE," a musical at their church.

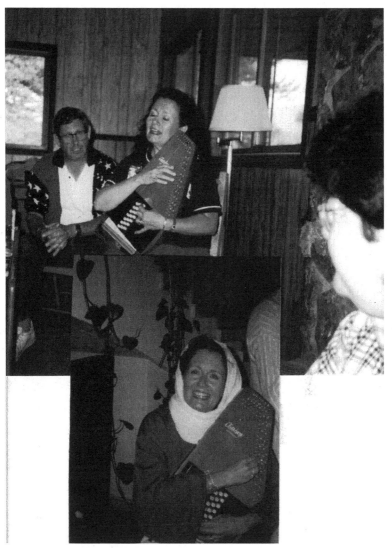

Judy is leading worship (top pic) before they dressed for
their performance at Estes Park, Colorado. Dean & the other
Michigan/Ohio Choir members, with Thurlow Spurr's (our
director) daughter, Vicki, looking on (right side of pic). Judy
is singing worship songs (bottom pic) with the MI/OH Choir
in the lobby of the hotel in Israel (with permission), when her
& Dean went to be part of Jerusalem 3000 event, in 1996.

Judy and Dean are singing hymns at the Fountain Square
in Nuremberg, Germany, when they went to visit their son,
Tony, serving in the Army there. Their daughter-in-law also
went with them and they were engaged in a beautiful park in
Germany, in 1988.

Judy is standing in front of one of the oldest Orthodox Cathedrals in Russia, when her & Dean went with the MI/ OH Choir, 5 days after the walls came down in 1991. They passed out Russian New Testaments & their choir was the first Gospel Choir to ever be allowed to sing in the Kremlin!

Judy is singing and speaking at Pastor Randy & Nancee Carter's church in Henderson, KY, at a Ladies Weekend Retreat. He was their former pastor in Ohio.

Judy with her older sister, Joyce, who went to heaven at 37 years old, in front of our home place near Pemberville, OH.

SOMETIMES HE SAYS WAIT

The sun was peeking through the trees,
On the first day of spring…
It made my heart glad
I wanted to sing.

Sing a song of thanks
To our awesome God
For soon His flowers
Will be pushed through the sod.

Winter's over, lilacs scent
Will fill the air…
If we look to Jesus
He will answer every care.

Sometimes He says wait
And other times its no…
Trust in His plan
Even though it may be slow.

My soul, wait though only upon God; for my expectation is from him.

Psalm 62:5

O thou that hearest prayer, unto thee shall all flesh come.

Psalm 65:2

STAY IN HIS TRUE WORD

When you look down the road of life, what do you see
Do you see selfish goals or God's hand setting free.

The only way we can succeed, is asking of the Lord
He will help us make the choice that we can afford.

Material things will pass away...
But eternal things are here to stay.

So when you see the path ahead
Do not be filled with dread.

Let God be there as your faithful guide
Stay in His true Word, each day abide.

Thy Word is a lamp unto my feet and a light unto my path.
Psalm 119:105

But seek ye first the kingdom of God and His righteousness
and all these things shall be added unto you.
Matthew 6:33

TAKING EACH STEP

Many footprints in the sand
People walking hand in hand.

With every step they make their choice
Will they heed God's call or their own voice?

Will they follow on the narrow way
Taking each step with a will to obey?

Or will they walk the road that's wide
Taking steps that are filled with pride.

Someday like a bird, they will fly away
We pray that they're ready for that day.

Choose you this day whom you will serve; as for me and
my house, we will serve the Lord.

Joshua 24:15

For even hereunto were you called: because Christ also
suffered for us an example, that we should follow His steps.

1 Peter 2:21

THANKSGIVING IS A CHOICE

The autumn leaves have fallen
Soon there will be snow.
God promised that seasons
Would surely come and go.

The sun will set and rise each day
So let your heart rejoice...
If truly makes a difference
Thanksgiving is a choice.

There's softness in that sunset
I love to see the hue...
Every one is different
With a sky of blue.

The barn is a reminder
Of labor that's been done
It's always harvest time
In our walk with God's Son.

Whoso offereth praise glorifieth me: and to him that ordereth his conversation aright will I shew the salvation of God.

Psalm 50:23

Pray ye therefore the Lord of the harvest, that he will send forth laborers into his harvest.

Matthew 9:38

THE JOY OF JESUS

Springtime is coming, it's not far away
The grass will be green, more sunshine each day.

But for now I'll be happy when the sun is hiding
Inside our home, with fireplace and lighting.

The joy of Jesus warms my heart
If I read His Word, we'll find a part.

A part that will comfort and help us grow
Forgiveness to wash us white as snow.

For the joy of the Lord is your strength.

Nehemiah 8:10b

Thou art my hiding place and my shield: I hope in Thy
Word.

Psalm 119:114

THERE'S JOY INSIDE

When we start our day the sunrise to see
We can have peace, truly it will be.

If we get our face into God's Book
Our faith will grow, take time to look.

It's a letter to us for our direction
When we heed God's word's we find protection.

There's joy inside that lifts our spirit
We must take time to daily hear it.

Let your tender mercies come unto me, that I may live: for your law is my delight. Plead my cause, and deliver me: restore life in me according to your word. Great are your tender mercies, O Lord: restore life in me according to your judgments.

Psalm 119:77, 154, 156

TODAY COULD BE THE DAY

I long to hear the robin's sweet song
After snow and storm; it sees so long

When the sun shines more and skies are blue
My heart reaches out to see tulips with dew.

Springtime is awesome when it comes in your heart
Only Jesus can bring new birth; His part.

If you don't know Him, today could be the day
Ask Him to forgive your sin and love Him, I pray.

And they said, Believe on the Lord Jesus Christ, and thou
shalt be saved, and thy house.

Acts 16:31

The Lord is my strength and song, and is become my
salvation.

Psalm 118:14

TRUST IN HIS MERCY

I love God's creation; the sand & the sea...
The cliffs and the mountains, the grass and each tree.

My eyes are drawn to the seagulls in the sky
So smoothly floating in the air, as they fly.

They do all they can to find their provision
But it's God who takes care of them; it's His decision.

He cares for each bird, how much more cares for you
We need to trust God; He's tried and true.

He'll see us through the trials at hand...
Trust in His mercy, He does understand.

But my God shall supply all your need according to His riches in glory by Christ Jesus.

Philippians 4:19

Trust in the Lord with all thine heart; and lean not unto thine own understanding.

Proverbs 3:5

TRUST IN THE LORD

The ocean waves are beautiful, refreshing and free
Giving us joy as we walk by the sea.

But then there are times that the waves are crashing
Bringing us fear with their roaring and thrashing.

When Jesus is near and says, "Peace be still."
All we can do is ask for His will.

Sometimes He will calm us in our storm…
Other times He will turn it from its form.

Our timing is different in every way
Trust in the Lord for the battle each day.

Though I walk in the midst of trouble, thou wilt revive me;
thou wilt stretch forth thine hand against the wrath of mine
enemies and Thy right hand shall save me.

Psalm 138:7

Fear thou not, for I am with thee; Be not dismayed, for I
am thy God. Yea I will strengthen thee, Yea I will help thee,
Yea I will uphold thee with the right hand of My righteouness.

Isaiah 41:10

TUNE YOUR EAR

When we say goodbye to another day
Another tomorrow; we don't know the way.

But we know the Lord, will hold our hand
He's always there to help us stand.

Each day is a promise that the Lord has for you
He knows what is best and His love is so true.

His voice is calling for you and for me
Forever He leads to help set us free.

So tune your ear to hear His voice
Follow His Word, to make the right choice.

Blessed are they that keep His testimonies, and that seek Him with the whole heart. They also do no iniquity, they walk in His ways.

Psalm 119:2, 3

And the sheep hear His voice: and He called His own sheep by name, and leadeth them out.

John 10:3b

WALK CLOSE TO GOD

When you look around in God's creation
It helps to use imagination
Sometimes many dark clouds are sent
Even the trees you see are bent.

The sparkling water, the grass so green
Overshadow the days that are very lean.
Some days are testing and boring at best
If our first love is Jesus, He helps pass each test.

God sees each purpose and every plan
We just see with eyes of man...
Walk close to God, stay in His Word.
His instruction will be the best you've heard.

Cast not away therefore your confidence, which hath great recompence of reward. For ye have need of patience, that after ye have done the will of God, ye might receive the promise.

Hebrews 10:35, 36

How ye ought to walk and to please God, so ye would abound more and more.

1 Thessalonians 4:1b

WHAT IS CHRISTMAS

Christmas brings joy & much imagination
If we know it's true meaning it brings
transformation
So long ago in a manger of hay
Jesus was born on Christmas Day.

That's why we celebrate that's why we sing
He came to die our salvation to bring...
So open your heart, confess your sin
He will bring great joy & peace within.

FOR UNTO US A CHILD IS BORN UNTO US A
SON IS GIVEN AND THE GOVERNMENT SHALL BE
UNPON HIS SHOULDER & HIS NAME SHALL BE
CALLED,WONDERFUL COUNSELOR, THE MIGHTY
GOD, THE EVERLASTING FATHER, THE PRINCE OF
PEACE

ISAIAH 9:6

WHAT IS THANKSGIVING

Thanksgiving is a matter of the heart
If your heart is focused, that can be a start.

If you believe in Jesus and that He died for YOU
It will then be overflowing, like a rose strewn with dew.

You will have that certain fragrance that some will enjoy
A thankful heart brings happiness and effervescent joy.

Others will wonder why you usually wear a grin
It'll be an open door to invite someone in.

Bring them in and tell them how to have a thankful heart
With your life's testimony, God will do the other part.

The happiest people are those who do His will
Read His Word; be thankful and your heart will be filled.

By Him therefore let us offer the sacrifice of praise to God continually, that is, the fruit of our lips giving thanks to His Name.

HEBREWS 13:15

That ye should shew forth the praises of Him who hath called you out of darkness into His marvelous light;

I PETER 2:9B

WHEN LIFE IS HARD

How wonderful it is to see the sunset on a body of water so
   clean
It touches our hearts with a peaceful feeling, so very calm and
   serene.

God is so good to care about us, to give us beauty to see...
Everything created so bountifully was planned for you and
   for me.

So take those times to look into the sky, or into a flower's face
It will remind us of God's love and His kind, unending grace.

When life is hard and you feel totally alone...
Ask Jesus to heal your heart, He's forever on His throne.

He's at the right hand of the Father, praying for you & I
He'll come into your heart, if you repent and draw nigh.

Before the mountains were brought forth, or ever, You
had formed the Earth and the world, even from everlasting to
everlasting, You are God.

                                        Psalm 90:2

Our soul waits for the Lord: He is our help and our shield
                                        Psalm 33:20

WHEN YOU ARE DOWN & OUT

When you are down & out & hope seems far away
Lift your eyes to heaven; He'll surely make a way.

His care for you is greater than you can understand
God wants to help in trials, so reach & take His hand.

He'll be there to comfort & to wipe away your tears
Take time to read His Word, it helps with all your fears.

Take time to pray for others, it gets self off your mind
Others are worse off, you know, so take the time; be kind.

I will lift up mine eyes unto the hills, from whence cometh my help, my help cometh from the Lord, who made heaven and earth.

Psalm 121:1, 2

Beloved, let us love one another; for love is of God; and everyone that loveth is born of God, and knoweth God.

1 John 4:7

WHEN YOU FEEL EMPTY

When you are dry
With no water to drink
You feel so empty
You can't even think.

Your heart has been broken
No hope in sight...
My faith is weak
It doesn't seem right.

So spiritually dry
Because of sad news
It will take some digging
To fight off the blues.

So I'll dig in God's Word
To fill my cup...
He's there to comfort
If I just look up.

I will lift mine eyes unto the hills, from whence cometh my help. My help cometh from the Lord which made heaven and earth.

Psalm 121:1, 2

Let not your heart be troubled: ye believe in God, believe also in me.

John 14:1

WHEN YOU PUT THE LORD FIRST

When your heart has been tried
And you've failed the test.

Come to the Lord
For His grace is the best.

If your hope is in Jesus
Nothing else matters

Everything pales
The enemy scatters.

You keep things in balance
When you put the Lord first.

Even in draught...
He'll quench your thirst.

For the Lord God is a sun and shield: the Lord will give grace and glory: no good thing will he withhold from them that walk uprightly.

Psalm 84:11

But seek ye first the kingdom of God, and His righteousness; and all these things shall be added unto you.

Matthew 6:33

YOU CAN GO TO THE BIBLE

Life brings much joy, but sorrows for sure
When we need comforting, the Lord has the cure.

You can go to the Bible anytime day or night
God's Word will bring comfort to help in the fight.

Each day is a battle we're surely to win
God's Son won the battle, He freed us from sin!

And God is able to make all grace abound toward you; that ye, always having all sufficiency in all things, may abound to every good work:

11 Corinthians 9:8

So then faith cometh by hearing, and hearing by the Word of God.

Romans 10:17

YOU GO TO YOUR KNEES

At times in our lives there is a stone wall
You feel that your heart is very small.

No open doors to fill a need
Nothing happening with any speed.

You go to your knees, to God you cry out
He then will help you not to pout.

He is the one that opens the gate
He's never too early or too late.

So Go to God's Word for guidance today
He is waiting there to help in the fray.

Trust and obey where you are right now
He'll work it out, though you don't know how.

If any of you lack wisdom, let him ask of God, who gives
to all men liberally, and upbraideth not; and it shall be given
him.

James 1:5

Give me understanding, and I shall keep Your Law; yea, I
shall observe it with my whole heart.

Psalm 119:34

YOU'LL FIND THE SEED

When you look at the world at it's hectic pace
You want to slow down; find a peaceful place.

When so many problems crowd your mind
Look to God's Word, your peace to find.

He has an answer for every need
In His presence you'll find the seed...

The seed that will grow and fill your heart
Just obeying God's Word will be your part.

But the meek shall inherit the earth; and shall delight themselves in the abundance of peace.

Psalm 37:11

Now the God of hope fill you with all joy and peace in believing, that ye abound in hope, through the power of the Holy Ghost.

Romans 15:13

YOUR WONDERFUL FACE I SEEK

The first day of fall has come
Beautiful day; new season to spawn.
Not knowing what lies ahead…
Trusting the Lord should be no dread.

A starting of this new fall week
Lord, Your wonderful face I seek.
You help me trust You; see every tear
With You by my side, I have nothing to fear.

We are happy in Jesus, at end of day
His Word is our comfort in the fray…
The Lord is my shepherd, want I shall not
He's always there in every hard spot.

But rather seek ye the kingdom of God; and all these things
shall be added unto you.

Luke 12:31

The Lord is my shepherd, I shall not want.

Psalm 23:1